SOFTBALL PITCHING FUNDAMENTALS AND TECHNIQUES

Carie Dever-Boaz
Sally Tippett Rains

COACHES CHOICE

ISBN: 1-57167-142-0
Library of Congress Catalog Card Number: 97-67169

Cover Design: Dody Bullerman
Cover Photo: Jon VerHoever
Production Manager: Michelle A. Summers

Coaches Choice Books is a division of: Sagamore Publishing, Inc.
P.O. Box 647
Champaign, IL 61824-0647
Web Site: http//www.sagamorepub.com

DEDICATION

I would like to dedicate this book to my Grama Irene and my Popa Max MacMillan for all of their undivided attention and loyal support throughout the years. They were both there for my first pitch and were two of my biggest and loudest fans. My Popa only saw me throw one year before God gave him the best seat at the ball park. My Grama rarely missed a game and always believed in me. I thank you both for always loving me no matter what the outcome of the game!

Carie Dever-Boaz

I dedicate this book to Rob, Mike, and B.J., who mean the world to me, and to my three special nieces, Ruth, Joan, and Anne. Remember, you can do whatever you want to do. Never stop believing in yourselves.

Sally Tippett Rains

ACKNOWLEDGMENTS

I owe a debt of gratitude to all those who invested their time, energy, and numerous hours in teaching me, showing me, and molding me into a pitcher. In particular, I would like to thank my father J.W. "Corky" Dever for the endless hours of squatting to catch and all of his bruised shins.

Doug Gove was instrumental in teaching me and many others how to pitch. He himself was an incredible pitcher who not only has the best knuckleball I have ever seen, but gave me enough information to learn to love to pitch and have a passion for the game. Margie Wright raised my skills to a level I did not know was possible during my career at Fresno State. She taught me many of the "how to's" of pitching, but most importantly, she gave me the knowledge and ability to teach and give back to our sport.

A special thanks to Joyce Compton for convincing me that college coaching and working with pitchers is where the Lord wanted me. She entrusted me with her entire pitching staff as a first year college coach.

Bruce Williams educated my team during its inaugural season and built my pitchers' strength to a level I never dreamed possible in three years. His insight in strength and conditioning has provided vital information for this book that I never could have put together on my own.

I would never be where I am today if not for all those young pitchers who were both eager and patient enough to work with me as their coach. They taught me more than they will ever know. I have enjoyed watching many of them go to college and succeed.

I would like to express my deepest gratitude to Sally Rains for all of her time and priceless advice. This book would not be possible without you, and I admire you for all of your insight.

Last, and certainly not least, to my mother, Zanita, husband, Bruce, and son, Max. My mother spent countless hours listening to ideas and reading and rereading the material in this book. My loving husband Bruce had to try to sleep through many nights with the lights on and deal with me popping out of bed to jot down another idea for the book. A very special thanks to my son for putting a smile on my face and laughter in my heart and constantly reminding me that this is truly just a game. The sun will come up tomorrow no matter who wins or loses.

CDB

Thanks to Carie for all of her work, and her prompt and professional way of doing things. I learned a lot, and I hope others enjoy the book as much as I enjoyed working with her. Thanks also to Sagamore Publishing and Peter Bannon for the opportunity.

STR

CONTENTS

Every softball play begins with a pitch. As such, even at younger age-level competition, the pitcher is often the key to a team's success. Accordingly, every coach should expect that at some time during her coaching career, she will be tasked to serve as her team's pitching coach. In that capacity, it will be her primary responsibility to help each of her pitchers develop to her fullest natural potential.

In this regard, the book was written to help coaches at all competitive levels determine what they should be looking for in their pitchers—physically, mentally, and emotionally. One of the duties of a coach is to identify those players who are best suited to be pitchers and provide them with the assistance to maximize their God-given talent. We have also attempted to provide a comprehensive overview of the fundamentals and techniques for throwing each of the basic pitches that a softball pitcher should have in her arsenal.

Not only are there different ways to grip the ball discussed, the book also presents a detailed review of when a pitcher should throw a particular pitch—based on the specific batter-and-game situation.

Throughout the book, the point is emphasized that a "right way" and a "wrong way" to do things while softball pitching do not always exist. As such, coaches should focus on taking the natural abilities of each pitcher and then building on those strengths. As a general rule of thumb, a coach should watch the way an athlete pitches and then try to improve the pitcher's methods and techniques, rather than completely change them. To the extent feasible, each pitcher should be allowed to develop her own sense of individuality—just as long as her individuality does not give rise to any undue problems with her pitching motion.

The book is designed to give pitchers the information that they need to progress to the next competitive level. Coaches should keep in mind that the "next level" can vary from one player to the next. As a result, coaches have a responsibility to decide what skills and drills are appropriate for an individual's age and experience level and act accordingly. Not surprisingly, what may be appropriate for an intercollegiate player would not necessarily be apropos for a youth softball player.

Finally, the book attempts to underscore the essential point that an athlete who wants to become an accomplished softball pitcher must be dedicated to the task. Her commitment must include an absolute resolve to learn as much as she can about the game by studying the game (through books and videos) and watching and observing more experienced athletes play the game. In this regard, she must also be willing to spend whatever time is necessary to practice (i.e., develop) her craft.

As individuals who sincerely love the game of softball, we wrote this book to help others—players and coaches alike—enjoy and appreciate this extraordinary sport. To the extent that we have accomplished this goal, then the effort to write this book will have been well worth it. As such, every softball enthusiasts who reads this book will hopefully adhere to the following advise—play ball, play hard, play safe, and have fun.

CDB
STR

CHAPTER 1

Softball—A Sport for Everyone

In recent years, softball has become increasingly popular. The 1996 United States Olympic team, led by shortstop Dot Richardson and an extraordinary pitching staff featuring Michelle Granger, Lisa Fernandez, and Michelle Smith, won a gold medal. In the process, the excitement of this incredible experience helped fuel widespread enthusiasm for the sport of softball. More than 40 million people participate in the sport today. In fact, it is the number one team participant sport in the United States. It will only increase in popularity as more and more youngsters take up the sport.

Those who are new to the sport of softball and believe it is "just baseball with a larger ball" will be completely surprised. The only thing softball really has in common with baseball is that it is played with a bat, a ball, and four bases. One of the largest differences between the two sports is the pitching technique. In baseball, the pitching is primarily overhand. In softball, it is underhand with a hard snap of the wrist. Even with the underhand delivery, premier softball pitchers can throw between 65-70 MPH. Not surprisingly, it can be very exciting to see an elite softball pitcher in action.

One of the most important things to remember when practicing softball and playing in games is to make the experience a positive one. Players should not let the business of trying to improve and perfect their game interfere with their enjoyment of it. In reality, softball, like other sports, is not a life-and-death situation. It is supposed to be fun. If a person learns more about something she loves doing and works hard to perfect her ability to engage in that activity, she will likely have more fun doing it. That is the spirit in which this book is written.

Another recurrent theme in this text is player safety. One of a coach's primary responsibilities is to keep her players safe. Hitters should wear the proper batting helmets, and pitchers should take precautions to ensure their safety. Stretching, warming up properly, and icing her pitching arm after workouts are a few areas that should become a regular habit for a pitcher.

It can also be very helpful for every softball player to know at least some history about the game. Softball began in November 1887 in Chicago, Illinois, at the Farragut Boat Club. It all started when the alumni of Yale and Harvard anxiously awaited the results of the Harvard versus Yale football game. Yale won that year, and an excited Yale supporter picked up an old boxing glove and threw it at a Harvard alumnus, who tried to hit it with a stick.

The throwing of that glove gave Chicago-resident George Hancock the inspiration for the sport of indoor baseball. By using all the equipment he could find lying around, he set up the predecessor of the softball field as it is known today in the Farragut Boat Club Gym. The first game ended with a score of 41-40. In the spring, Hancock took the sport outside and played it on fields too small for baseball. Hancock and his friends began challenging other gyms and gradually traveled throughout the country. Thanks to a fireman named Lewis Rober in Minneapolis, the sport flourished. He wanted something for his firemen to do during their idle time to keep fit, and softball was perfect. Soon the idea caught on at many other stations, and the first league was formed.

The name "softball" came from Walter Hakanson, a former ASA commissioner. His efforts were rewarded in 1933 when the sport gained acceptance by being tied to the Chicago World's Fair. Teams were divided into three categories—fast pitch, slow pitch, and women. The ball used was 14 inches in diameter.

The pitching rubber was originally placed 35 feet from home plate, but was eventually moved to 40 feet. In the NCAA today, the pitching distance is 43 feet. Although many rules in softball have changed over the years much more uniformity in the sport exists today. Most of the changes to pitching rules have been made in an attempt to create more offense, since many people believe offense is what keeps the fans interested.

CHAPTER 2

The Basics

One of the primary goals of every pitcher should be to reach the next level of competition. In that regard, the coach should help her pitchers achieve that objective by teaching them all she can about the physical, mechanical, and mental aspects of pitching. Many different teaching methods exist. The one used in this book is the philosophy of "chaining." Chaining is breaking a process down into pieces and then putting it back together.

USE HER NATURAL TALENT

People often think there is a right way and a wrong way to do something in sports. In softball, every pitcher can have her own individual style. As such, the coach should observe a pitcher to determine her strengths and then help her build on those strengths. The point to remember is that forcing a pitcher to emulate a specific pitcher usually keeps her from reaching her highest level. In reality, the same techniques do not work for everyone. Accordingly, coaches and pitchers should experiment with changes or suggestions to determine what works best for each individual.

The coach should have the pitcher go to the mound and throw to the catcher. She should watch the motion of the dance, the weight transfer, the hip rotation, the arm circle, the leg drive, the release, and the follow-through. The coach should keep in mind that there is no right way to do the dance. Every pitcher has her own version.

One of the best ways to learn is by first watching, and then doing. The beginning pitcher should watch many different pitchers. This step will help her decide what will work for her and what will not. If she is young but already has a pitching motion she is comfortable with, she may not need to change. She should first try to improve on what she has.

Much of a pitcher's success depends on her natural talent. Anyone can stand on the pitcher's mound and throw the ball to home plate, but it takes a special kind of person to be a pitcher. The focus of a pitcher should be to develop her natural abilities and skills to the highest level possible. In this regard, her coach should do all she can to help her.

Pitching involves many elements, including the throwing arm, the glove arm, the hips, and weight transfer. A pitcher must learn to make all those elements work together properly. A well-oiled machine has many parts that collectively perform a specific task; the same is true of a mechanically sound pitcher.

THROWING A PITCH

In softball, pitches are thrown underhand. Perhaps the best place to start is with a review of the basic fundamental and techniques involved in throwing a pitch.

Leg drive toward the target

The pitcher begins with her feet properly placed on the rubber, or pitcher's mound. Her hands begin the drive with either a rocking motion, in which the throwing hand will pass the driving leg before driving forward, or a pumping of the hands together while driving forward.

The short body movement and the arm swing is referred to as the dance. The dance is any rocking or pumping motion that happens before engagement towards the intended target. It is what helps each individual find her rhythm, begins the pitcher's drive toward home. The throwing arm should be loose and relaxed while whipping through a full circle.

When the step foot is planted after the kick, it should face approximately where one or two o'clock would be on a watch. As the throwing arm whips down towards the hip, which is also the release point, the hips should naturally rotate back to the original stance, facing the catcher. This action puts the pitcher in position to play defense.

THE SEQUENCE OF SUCCESSFUL PITCHING

#1. The Grip
The ball can be gripped in a variety of ways. The beginning pitcher should find one grip and stick with it. This will allow her to develop some feel for the seams as well as watch the rotation of the seams on the ball. Because a softball can be large to a young player with smaller hands, it is very important to find a comfortable grip. The beginning pitcher should not be concerned with many different grips; the focus should be on a good, fluid motion. Simplicity is best.

The seams on a softball form four horseshoes. As the pitcher grips the ball, it does not matter whether the horseshoe opens to the left or right, although many pitchers will develop a preference over time. The pitcher should place her fingers across the horseshoe with her fingertips on the seam. Her thumb should be on the underside horseshoe. However, many young pitcher's hands may be too small so make sure the young pitcher's thumb is on the underside even if they cannot reach seams. The coach should make sure the ball is not in the palm. There should always be an open air pocket. A pitcher should be able to feel her fingers and fingertips working. The easiest pitch for a beginner to learn is a peel drop.

Three-finger drop grip

When grips are explained in this book, the thumb is not counted as a finger; "two fingers" means "two fingers and the thumb." Some coaches teach a two-finger peel drop grip, in which the index and middle fingers are on the top of the ball across the horseshoe with the tips on the seam. Ideally, the thumb should be on the bottom seam in the middle of the two top fingers. Hand size will affect finger and thumb placement. A pitcher with small hands would struggle with a two-finger grip, but could use a three-finger peel drop grip, which places the index, middle, and ring fingers on top across the horseshoe. The thumb, underneath the ball, is aligned with the middle finger. The coach may teach her pitchers to keep either their little finger on the side of the ball for balance or keep it tucked. The four-finger peel drop grip is used by most younger players or players with small hands. In this grip, the pitcher places the thumb on the bottom of the ball and all four fingers on top. The pitcher should work toward a three-finger or two-finger peel drop to increase the movement of the ball.

Two-finger drop grip

#2. Foot Placement

Different leagues may allow different pitching stances. The one taught in this book places both feet in contact with the rubber, a practice which adheres to college rules.

The pitcher should begin by placing both feet in contact with the rubber. The stride foot (the left foot if the pitcher is right-handed), should just barely touch the back edge of the rubber. The

Proper placement of feet on mound

heel of the push-off foot (the right foot) should be on the front 1-3 inches of the rubber. This stance provides a good base for balance, which is essential to starting a successful delivery.

The dance is rocking motion that occurs before the delivery is started

#3. The Dance

The dance is the rocking motion a pitcher does before starting her delivery that gets her to the driving motion toward the catcher. All factors considered, pitchers should develop their own dance so their personality comes out in their pitching. It should be remembered that the same things do not work for everyone; if a pitcher's dance helps her find her own rhythm, it is correct. She should use whatever helps her attain the maximum drive into her delivery. A dance should be a personal comfort zone; all pitchers need not look alike, nor is there one correct way to do it.

#4. Balance

One reason each pitcher should develop her own dance is the need to maintain and control her balance. Balance is very important in pitching, from the beginning of the foot placement to the follow-through. If a pitcher is even slightly off-balance, her delivery will be affected. If a pitcher is continually off-balance, it will be very difficult for her to learn how to successfully throw different pitches.

#5. Weight transfer

Weight transfer from the push-off leg to the stride leg is critical to power and speed. A right-handed pitcher pushes off with her right leg and transfers her weight to her left leg. The coach can have a pitcher jog slowly to feel the weight transfer taking place between the legs. The same basic process is taking place in pitching. Lateral power is important because the pitcher is driving forward. Incorrect weight transfer in hitting can set a hitter up for failure. The same is true in pitching.

Each pitcher should develop her own dance

Beginning right-handed pitchers should rock with most of their weight on or over their left leg. They should push their weight to the right leg (push-off leg) and drive forward on their stride leg. The transfer of weight back to the step foot completes the pitching motion.

#6. Hip rotation

Though the hips rotate during the pitching motion, they should begin and end square to the catcher. The opening and closing of the hips should be a natural occurrence. The pitcher should put her hands on her hips and push off as if she is pitching the ball. If she drives toward the catcher as hard as she can, she should feel her hips naturally rotate open. As the throwing arm whips forward, the hips should rotate back toward a closed position. However, if the pitcher does not use her hips as a release point and then follow through, her hips might not close completely.

#7. The Drive

The drive involves all of the power collected from the ground up through the legs to the arm and on to the ball. Basketball players, when rebounding, bend at the knees to maximize their drive up off the ground. The same principle applies in pitching, except that the pitcher is driving out rather than up. Ninety percent of all power and speed comes from the drive. The other ten percent is a combination of timing, body size, and natural talent.

Leg drive forward

Power line extender

#8. Stride and Foot plant

The stride out should occur naturally just before the wrist snaps to release the ball. Beginning pitchers may have problems with striding too far to the right or left. They should drive out directly toward their catcher, although this action will change somewhat when they begin learning to throw new pitches and hit targets. If a pitcher's stride is too long, her shoulders will start to dip to one side. If her stride is too short, she is not driving as hard as she can. She should imagine that she is trying to reach out and grab her catcher.

On the drive, all players and coaches should be aware of the power line. The power line extends about five feet in front of the pitcher from the inside of her drive foot. After she has driven toward home, her plant foot should be in line with the power line. When she plants her foot, it should end up on the power line at about one or two o'clock. Many young pitchers will plant their foot at about three o'clock. This makes it very hard to throw different pitches and also puts a lot of pressure on the knee, setting them up for problems later. If a pitcher plants at 12 o'clock, she did not rotate her hips or drive as hard as she can towards her intended target. As a result, she never reached her maximum drive.

#9. Release
The release is the point at which the ball actually leaves the pitcher's hand and fingers. The pitcher should use a quick snapping motion of the wrist when releasing the ball. Her hips should once again be facing the catcher. The release point is a small box in the hip area, approximately six to eight inches in length and five to seven inches in width. The ball needs to be released in this area in order to throw a strike.

The release involves a quick snap of the wrist

Follow-through

#10. Follow-through
After releasing the ball, the pitcher needs a good follow-through in order to be in the proper position to play defense. The pitcher should be prepared for the batter to make contact on every pitch. The pitcher should end up with her hips once again square to the catcher. No matter how she follows through, the pitcher should maintain her balance in order to be capable of fielding a ball if the situation requires it.

BREAKING IT DOWN INTO TWO PHASES

After breaking the pitching process down into pieces, it is important to put it all back together to help the pitcher understand the concept of mechanically sound pitching. The entire sequence can be divided into two segments—Phase I and Phase II.

Phase I is the foot placement on the mound, the dance, the initial drive toward the catcher, the extension of the arms toward the plate, and the natural hip rotation that occurs and places the driving foot on the power line.

Phase II is made up of the whip of the throwing arm toward the release point, the glove arm pulling down toward the hip, the hip rotation, the final drive to the release of the ball, and the follow-through.

Once a pitcher has begun to master the art of pitching, it is important to have a reference point from which to analyze her mechanics. The breaking down of the pitching motion into Phase I and Phase II can provide that reference point for the pitcher and her coach.

Phase I

Phase II

CHAPTER 3

Throwing Different Pitches

No one correct way exists to hold or grip the ball to throw various pitches. Many different grips are used for each pitch. The point to remember is that each pitcher should use the one that feels and works the best for her. Movement on the ball depends more on a quick and correct wrist snap than on the grip on the ball. Some grips help maximize seam use, which in turn increases rotation of the ball and allows the ball to achieve more movement.

THE CHANGE-UP

Every pitcher should first develop a change-up. Most batters will struggle more with different ball speeds than with different ball movement, since different speeds from 40 or 43 feet can be hard for a batter to detect. The change-up is also an easier pitch to master than some of the other pitches because it does not interfere with a young pitcher's development of a mechanically sound delivery. Several different types of change-up pitches can be taught, including the palmball, the circle change, and the knuckleball.

Palmball grip

The correctly thrown palmball contradicts one pitching fundamental: the ball should be held in the palm of the hand with no air pocket. This pitch is the only one in which the fingertips are not used to grip the ball.

When throwing a palmball, or any other change-up, a pitcher must understand that she should not slow down her pitching motion. If she does, the pitch is set up for failure before the ball ever leaves her hand. In order to not slow down her pitching motion, she should imagine her legs weighing an extra 50 pounds or feeling as if she has already thrown three or four games. The legs should feel heavy and lazy.

When releasing the palmball, the pitcher should push the ball from the pad of her hand. The coach may ask the pitcher to shotput the ball so she can feel it leave her palm. No matter how hard the pitcher tries to throw this pitch, it should float to home because she has removed the air pocket and thrown or pushed it from her palm.

The circle change is not particularly difficult to master. Many pitchers, however, will first feel as if they do not have a good grip on the ball. The grip is similar to the peel drop, which makes it easy for the beginning pitcher to adjust to this pitch. When throwing the circle change, the pitcher should place her fingers across the seam as for the peel drop, then form a circle on the side of the

Circle change grip

ball with her index finger and thumb. The middle, ring, and little fingers remain spread across the horseshoe. Once again, the pitcher's legs should feel heavy or lazy, while her motion and movement speed are the same as for any other pitch. When the pitcher releases the ball, she should feel it roll off the three fingers placed across the horseshoe.

The location of a change-up plays a large part in whether or not it is successful. It should be at the batter's knees or lower and cross the inside or outside corner of the plate. If a pitcher keeps the change-up in the correct location, the batter will have a relatively hard time doing any damage even if she makes contact with the ball.

Several different schools of thought exist as to when a pitcher should use the change-up. Some coaches believe it should be used later in the game, but a pitcher with an extremely effective change-up may want to use it early in the game. The decision should be based on the pitcher's ability to throw the change-up and her confidence in it. She should be comfortable enough with the change-up to throw it as a first pitch or with a full count. On the other hand, she should not develop a pattern of throwing it or the batter will sit back and wait for it.

The change-up can be a very effective strike-out pitch. The pitcher can acquire good control of her change-up and build her confidence by throwing to actual batters in practice. Coaches can teach the pitcher what pitch to throw in different situations.

Among the situations for which it is particularly appropriate to throw a change-up are the following:

- When the batter is pulling the ball.
- When the batter is overstriding.
- When the hitter has any type of hand or arm movement.
- To set up another pitch.
- Throw off a hitter's timing.

THE KNUCKLEBALL

Many pitchers use a knuckleball as a change-up because it is a relatively slower pitch. A knuckleball, however, is more effective if it is accompanied with another good change-up. Pitchers should be aware that the knuckleball is very difficult to control.

A good knuckleball will typically keep a pitcher and a catcher in suspense as to what direction it will break. Ideally, a knuckleball has no seam rotation when the ball leaves the pitcher's hand. As a result, when the wind hits the seams of the ball, the pitch may drop, rise, or break left or right.

With regard to throwing a knuckleball, some coaches teach pitchers to curl their fingers all the way to the knuckle. Some pitchers may find it easier to dig the fingertips of the ring, middle, and index fingers into the ball between the two horseshoes instead. The fingers bring the ball back into the pad of the hand while the thumb and little finger are on either side.

Knuckleball grip

The pitcher's wrist should be locked throughout the delivery and release, so there is no movement or wrist snap on the release. The coach may tape a pitcher's hand and wrist so she can feel any wrist movement made in the release. When the pitcher's arm reaches the release point, it should come to a quick stop as if hitting a wall. At this point, the pitcher should push the ball off all the fingers at the same time.

One of the best ways to learn to throw the knuckleball is to start working from a short distance. The pitcher should stand as close to her target as is necessary for her to throw the ball with no rotation. Once she masters it at that distance, she should gradually increase the distance to her target. She should be able to feel all of her fingers leaving the ball at the same time. Even young pitchers may start learning this pitch. Most of them will enjoy learning something new and working on something besides basic mechanics. Pitchers should understand it can take anywhere from two months to more than two years to learn this pitch. The key is learning how to push all the fingers off at one time, while the arm hits a wall at the release point. The arm does not stop completely at the hip; it is really a quick hesitation that occurs when the ball leaves the hand. This momentum will then carry the arm forward.

THE DROP BALL

The drop ball is a useful pitch because it changes planes on the batter. It begins on one plane and drops into another. A young pitcher should start with a peel drop because it only involves peeling the fingertips off the seams, not an over the top wrist snap like the over-the-top drop. Both pitches are effective. As a pitcher advances, however, she should learn to use the over-the-top drop because it creates more ball movement.

The grip is the same for both pitches. A pitcher may place two, three, or four fingers across the horseshoe. The thumb is on the bottom of the ball, preferably in the middle of the ball. Pitchers with small hands, however, may not be able to reach this far. The thumb should be turned on its side, not flat against the ball. This position helps create an air pocket between the ball and the palm and keeps the ball from resting too far back in the palm.

For the peel drop, the pitcher should pull the fingers off the ball with a quick wrist snap. The pitcher's stride should be shorter in order to attain a good angle on top of the ball. For the over-the-top drop, a pitcher should try to throw her thumb to the ground during the wrist snap. Beginning pitchers should start by throwing their thumb to the opposite leg, then through the legs, and then finally work up to

Air pocket for the drop ball grip

throwing the thumb to the ground beside the drive leg. The pitcher should shorten her stride so she is pitching with her chest over her toes. This angle should not be achieved by bending at the hips or pushing the buttocks out backwards. Many young pitchers struggle with taking a shorter stride. The coach should try instructing them to get their chest angled over their toes. This action will help shorten their stride. The wrist snap should occur as quickly as possible.

Among the situations for which it is particularly appropriate to throw a drop ball are the following:

- When the hitter is holding her hands too high.
- When the batter is bailing out of the strike zone or box.
- When the batter is standing in the back of the box.
- When the game situation calls for an infield ground ball.
- When the batter is a "slapper" who takes her first step toward the plate.

Body angle on top of the ball for the drop ball

THE RISE BALL

The rise ball, like the drop ball, is an extremely effective pitch because it changes planes. It should be taught after both a change-up and a drop ball have been mastered.

Several different grips can be used for the rise ball. The most fairly common grip involves having the pitcher place her middle finger and

Rise ball grip

ring finger on the rounded top seams of the horseshoes. Her index finger should be tucked on the side. How much the pitcher tucks her index finger will depend on her hand size and the level of ball security. The point to be emphasized is that she should tuck it as far as she can within her comfort zone. She should apply as much pressure with her index finger as she can. If she is doing it correctly, the side of her finger by her nail will be sore after pitching when she is first starting out with this pitch. Ideally, the pitcher's thumb should be on the bottom of the ball between her middle and ring fingers.

The pitcher should stride out as far as she can without losing her balance. The rise ball has the longest stride of any of the pitches. A common mistake pitchers make is leaning over the ball when trying to get under it to snap. To get under the ball, the pitcher should use a long stride and bend her drive knee. She should feel her stomach muscles working and feel as though she is pulling her shoulders back. She should snap her wrist as if she is turning a door knob as fast as she can getting full rotation by throwing her thumb to the ground from a hitch-hiking position. If she has rotated her wrist and forearm as far as they can go, she has thrown the pitch correctly.

Among the situations for which it is particularly appropriate to throw a rise ball are the following:

- When the batter is up in the box.
- When the batter has her hands pulled in tight.
- When the batter is crowding the plate.
- When the batter is overstriding.
- When a bunt is suspected.

Curve ball wrist snap

THE CURVE BALL

The curve ball is essentially a lazy rise ball. Although the curve does not necessarily change planes, it moves from right to left from a right-handed pitcher and left to right from a left-hander. The curve helps set up the rise and drop balls and can make them more effective.

The curve ball can be thrown with the same grip as the rise ball. To practice the wrist snap, a pitcher should work on throwing a Frisbee backwards with her palm facing up. When she can make the Frisbee fly, she has learned the proper wrist snap for the curve. The palm should face up after the wrist snap, not down.

As the pitcher's arm whips toward the release point, the elbow should be driving down toward the hip, as if being pulled by a string. The arm should maintain a full extended circle and not bend at the elbow.

The stride for the curve ball is not as long as the rise ball and not as short as the drop ball. The pitcher should have a good comfortable leg drive. Her hips should close sharply immediately following her wrist snap.

Among the situations for which it is particularly appropriate to throw a curve ball are the following:

- When a left-handed batter is crowding or stepping into the plate.
- When the batter is standing away from the plate.
- When the hitter is lunging or sweeping at the ball.
- When the pitcher wants the batter to hit the ball to the right side.
- When the batter is a "slapper" who takes her first step toward the plate.
- When the batter steps away from the plate.

THE SCREW BALL

The screw ball can be very damaging physically to a pitcher if it is not thrown correctly. Although it can be an effective pitch, a pitcher needs to be fully developed before learning to throw the screwball. This pitch should be learned with the assistance of a pitching coach so the coach can immediately make any necessary changes to the pitcher's mechanics to avoid stress on her arm and elbow.

This book will describe two different grips for the screwball. The first is called the Mork and Mindy (Nanu) grip. When using the Nanu grip, the pitcher places the index and middle fingers together on one top-rounded horseshoe seam, and the ring and little fingers together on the opposite rounded horseshoe seam. The thumb grips the bottom seam and splits the "V" created by the four fingers. The splitting of the fingers allows the pitcher to get a good feeling for the cutting of the ball off the fingertips.

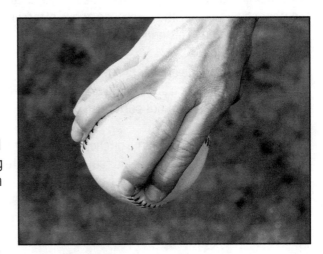

Screw ball grip

Step away to let the arm come through on the screw ball

The other grip is also very effective. The pitcher should place all four of her fingers together on one side of the horseshoe, while stretching her thumb as far as possible to the bottom seam. This grip forms a large round "C" on the side of the ball.

The wrist snap and the arm motion of the screw ball are like an inside-out curve. By going through the motion slowly, the pitcher can see that the screw ball can put a lot of stress on the arm if not performed correctly.

When throwing a screw ball, the pitcher's step is not to the power line, but about eight inches to the side. She should feel as if she is stepping in a bucket. This action is necessary to clear the hips out of the way for the arm and the wrist snap to come through. The pitcher should still drive hard so she does not lose too much speed, since the screwball is already a slower pitch because of the body motion and the stride.

Many of the basics of pitching are contradicted when throwing the screw ball. On no other pitch is the pitcher told to step away from the power line and the target and move her hips completely out of the way to let the arm come through. A pitcher should start slowly when learning to throw the screw ball and stop immediately if she feels any stress or pain in her elbow or shoulder.

Among the situations for which it is particularly appropriate to throw a screw ball are the following:

- When a batter is a "slapper."
- When a batter is bunting.
- When a batter uses a closed stance or struggles with an inside pitch.
- When a batter sweeps at the ball or goes long to the ball.
- When a batter crowds the plate.

PRACTICING DIFFERENT PITCHES

Being able to throw a rise ball, a drop ball, a curve ball, a screw ball, or a change-up takes a lot of practice and determination. The hard work is worth it when a pitcher begins to experience success with her pitches.

Pitchers should enjoy the challenge of learning to throw new pitches and remember not to expect to perfect any of them in a day or even a week. All of these pitches can add a lot to a pitcher's game, especially rise balls and drop balls because they change planes. The pitcher should work primarily on the spins of a pitch before she expects to see movement from the mound. The pitcher and her coach should break the pitch down into the grip, the wrist snap and the stride and work on mastering each step. She should then put the entire sequence together to begin mastering the pitch and movement.

CHAPTER 4

Details Can Make the Difference

GET TO KNOW THE CATCHER

It is important for a pitcher and her catcher to develop a good relationship. Literally, they are a team within a team. If they know each other well, they will be better able to help each other. There should be mutual respect and trust so they can discuss relevant matters, disagree as the situation arises, and try different ways of doing things.

Because every play begins with a pitch, it is important for the pitcher to be comfortable with the skills and thought processes of the catcher. Eventually, the pitcher and the catcher must begin to think as one unit on the field. The lines of communication must be open between the two of them both on the field and in the dugout. Pitchers should remember the catcher can see things that they may not, such as how a batter is standing in the box, how tense a batter is, or maybe even what the batter is planning to do during her turn at bat. If she and her catcher can become one unit on the field, the pitcher may be able to reach competition levels she never thought possible.

DEVELOP A GOOD RELATIONSHIP WITH THE UMPIRE

A special relationship can also be formed between the pitcher and the umpire. Such a relationship should also be formed between the catcher and the umpire. A pitcher should make sure her catcher has a good relationship and an open line of communication with the umpire. General conversation between the catcher and the umpire can help develop a good working relationship.

All players, especially pitchers, should remember that most umpires tend to like their jobs because they love the sport in a manner similar to the players. They are not out there calling the game simply for the money. Players do not like to be humiliated, made fun of, or embarrassed. Not surprisingly, neither does the umpire. Good relationships between the pitcher and the umpire, the catcher and the umpire, and the pitcher and the catcher can all be important to the success of a pitcher's game. Players should work hard to establish and keep these relationships and develop trust and respect between the individuals involved.

DEVELOP A GOOD COACH-PLAYER RELATIONSHIP

One of the most special relationships a pitcher can have is with her coach. The coach and pitcher must be able to trust each other. Good communication will help establish this important relationship.

A pitcher looks to the coach not only for help with mechanics, but also for advice in game situations. A coach should vary her pitcher's workouts on a regular basis and make sure she does not place undue stress on her pitcher's arms (e.g., use pitchers in place of a batting machine too often). The coach should also remember that the pitcher experiences success or failure on nearly every pitch. As such, she needs a lot of reinforcement of her progress and specific directions about what steps she needs to undertake to continue her progress as a pitcher.

Pitchers should not be catered to or treated delicately. Even though softball is a team sport, it also has many of the qualities of individual sports. Pitching and hitting, for example, are both very individual actions at that single moment in time. On the other hand, the pitcher has to have a defense behind her, and a hitter has to have someone to drive her in once she reaches base. When developing a good working relationship with her pitcher, a coach will also need to know when to pull a pitcher. Times will occur, however, when the coach should stay with a pitcher and let her find out if she can pitch out of a jam. It is also important to remember, however, that consideration of a pitcher's personal growth on the field should never jeopardize the team or the outcome of a game.

NEVER BE PREDICTABLE

Although pitchers should strive to be consistent, they should avoid being predictable. A pitcher becomes predictable when she begins falling into patterns. If not vigilant, pitchers can succumb to exhibiting certain tendencies while pitching, including always throwing a change-up with two strikes, always throwing the first pitch for a strike, and always throwing a specific pitch on the first pitch. These examples are just a few; there are many more. The point to remember is that any pitcher who falls into a pattern gives the hitter a substantial advantage if the hitters quickly figure out a pitcher's tendencies, the pitcher's likelihood of dominance is weakened. As such, the pitcher should always keep the hitters guessing. The only person who should know what a pitcher is going to do on the next pitch is her catcher.

LOCATION, LOCATION, LOCATION

Once a pitcher has mastered the different pitches, she should begin to work on throwing those pitches to different locations. It is rather easy to throw inside or outside—all the pitcher has to do is move her plant foot two inches either to the left or to the right on the power line. Changing her plant foot to either side of the power line will move the pitch inside and outside. In other words, "Where the leg and foot go, the body must follow."

Once a pitcher has learned to throw her drop ball, rise ball, and change-up inside and outside, she should begin experimenting with an inside and outside curve ball or a low rise ball. The screw ball is not a pitch the pitcher should try to throw outside. It is very important for a pitcher to be able to hit spots. If she has not learned certain pitches or is just in the process of developing them, she can rely on the fastball to hit specific locations.

CHAPTER 5

Mental Preparation and Toughness

The mental preparation of a pitcher can directly affect the outcome of a game. It also can directly affect the improvement of a pitcher, because a pitcher who mentally prepares prior to each workout moves a step closer to reaching her highest potential as an athlete.

When a pitcher changes into her uniform or practice clothes, she should feel as if she is entering another world. When a pitcher is pitching, there is nothing else in her life she can be doing at exactly the same time. Each part of a pitcher's life must be put into its correct compartment before she goes out to a practice or a game.

It is important for a coach to recognize each individual's own routine, beliefs, and approach to mental preparation and toughness. What works for the coach, for example, will not necessarily work for her pitcher. Just as players should be allowed to develop their own physical individuality, as long as it will not lead to future problems, they should be given the same freedom in developing their approach to mental preparation and toughness.

Visualization can be a critical mental skill for a pitcher. Such a technique is essential because if a pitcher can visualize a particular situation and its outcome before it actually occurs, she will have more experience in any given situation. For example, if a pitcher can visualize herself working pitch by pitch against a given batter, she can then recreate such a scenario when the situation actually arises.

Visualization is a great technique that can enable a pitcher to recognize and become aware of her anxieties or fears. For example, a coach can have pitchers close their eyes and give them a specific situation to visualize; she can then have them walk through it pitch by pitch to the preconceived outcome. Visualization, like physical skills, requires practice and repetition to improve. It is important to keep in mind that because younger pitchers tend to be more uncomfortable with the process of visualization, they may need more help from the coach.

Mental toughness is one of the key traits possessed by every successful pitcher. While it can be enhanced by visualization, it comes mostly from having a competitive spirit and a singular focus on succeeding. Ninety percent of all "fear" in softball is based on ignorance and the unknown, both of which players and coaches can control. As such, a pitcher should learn as much as she can about the art of pitching because, all factors considered, education destroys ignorance. Doing away with the unknown requires a lot of practice and a lot of engaging in actual games. A pitcher should practice all types of situations, both good and bad.

A coach can dedicate a portion of practice time every day to working on various situations. One way to do this is to put runners in different situations, bring up specific batters, and pitch one inning at a time featuring that scenario. The coach should try to address a wide variety of situations so that when a particular situation arises during a game, the pitcher has dealt with it before.

Among the scenarios that can be set up by the coach are the following:
- Runners at first and second; two outs; the clean-up hitter at the plate.
- Bases loaded; sixth inning; no outs; the pitcher's team leading by one run.
- Winning run at second; seventh inning; the batter is someone the pitcher has struggled with in the past.
- First inning; the lead-off hitter is a "slapper;" the second hitter is a powerful left-handed pull hitter; the third batter is right-handed.

A coach should look through game books and identify batters that her pitchers have struggled with and been successful against in the past. This process can enable her to be very creative when thinking of different situations to work on during practice. It also is important to have the pitcher pick out situations she would like to practice. This step allows her to work on whatever factors she considers her biggest weakness, which, in turn, will improve her level of mental preparation.

Another way to help make the pitcher become more comfortable with visualization is to have her lead the entire team through hitting and defensive visualization situations. This step can benefit not only the pitcher, but the entire team.

Several other aspects exist that enhance mental preparation and play a key role in mental toughness. Two of these factors are homework and identifying a hitter's weaknesses, both of which will be covered in detail in later chapters.

All factors considered, mental toughness and mental preparation improve the most when a pitcher sets goals and maps out a way to achieve those goals. A pitcher should have not only a daily plan of tasks she wants to accomplish, but also a weekly plan and a monthly plan—both for in-season and out-of-season periods. This step makes it easier for her to track her progress, prevent wasted time, and maintain high-quality practices.

It is also a good idea for a pitcher to take a few minutes after every practice to log in a journal the significant events of that practice (e.g., what she accomplished, what she needs to improve on, how well she stayed on task, what she could have done differently, etc.). She can then rate the workout on a scale of one to five, one being the best and five being the worst. Over a period of time, she can then adjust her personal approach to practicing as appropriate.

CHAPTER 6

Physical Preparation: In-Season and Out-of-Season Workouts

Training to become a successful pitcher involves more than just throwing "x" number of pitches and learning "x" number of new pitches. Players also have an obligation to prepare themselves physically. Such preparation ensures that each athlete will be able to effectively handle the physical demands imposed upon her body during competition. The point that should be emphasized in this regard is that the more physically fit the athlete is, the better able she will be to perform, the longer she will be able to sustain her performance at an optimal level, and the less likely she will suffer an on-the-field injury.

Accordingly, pitchers who want to maximize their performance capabilities and minimize their undue risk of being injured will engage in a properly designed, year-round conditioning program. Such a program will address the four basic components of physical fitness (i.e., muscular fitness, aerobic fitness, flexibility, and body composition), as well as provide a sufficient amount of actual throwing (pitching).

FIT TO WIN

Above all else, softball is a sport that involves muscular power and anaerobic conditioning (i.e., the ability to move the body in an intense manner without oxygen). Every swing of the bat, each explosive move to get to a ground ball hit in the gap, or every throw to the plate to keep a run from scoring requires muscular power. Sprinting to first base, running under a fly ball, and rounding second on the way to third all test the anaerobic conditioning of the softball athlete. Other important physical attributes inherent in the game are agility (the ability to change directions), foot speed and acceleration, flexibility (primarily involving the shoulders, low back, legs) and muscular endurance (shoulders). The pitcher and her coach should initially focus on how the pitcher should train to improve muscular power and anaerobic conditioning.

The conditioning programs in this chapter are based on information provided by Bruce Williams, the strength coach for the department of athletics for the University of Arkansas, and are provided for informational purposes only. Any coach or pitcher who decides to begin a conditioning program should contact qualified professional (e.g., an exercise science specialist; a NSCA-certified professional, etc.).

MUSCULAR FITNESS

The first component in training for successful power development is muscular strength. "Power" is made up of two things: strength and speed. Muscular strength is the foundation of being powerful. Strength is the ability of a muscle to exert force one time. As the muscle overcomes this resistance, it will become stronger. If it is not properly challenged, the muscle will not only stop getting stronger, it will actually get weaker. As a result, it is important to always strength train properly and to use the correct amount of resistance.

HOW MUSCLES WORK

Proper resistance training is designed to make a muscle get stronger, which in turn helps the muscle become more powerful. In reality, athletes are not training just the muscles themselves; they are also training the nerves connected to those muscles. The athlete should picture the muscles as an engine in a sports car and the nerves connected to those muscles as the gas pedal. Without a gas pedal, there would be no way of utilizing the strong engine. The nerves connect the brain to the muscles so that the muscles will do what the athlete wants them to. Just as an athlete conditions her muscles to be strong, she must also train the nerves to fire those strong muscles quickly. This application is the essence of power.

JUMPING EXERCISES

The use of plyometrics, or jumping exercises, is one highly popular method used to train for power. The primary objective of plyometric exercises is to make the nervous system recruit muscles to counteract resistance. This resistance is usually the athlete's body weight against gravity. To see how plyometrics can train the nervous and muscular systems, an athlete should stand next to a wall, then jump, taking note of how far up the wall she jumped. She should then take another jump, and, as soon as she lands, jump again. The final jump is often the highest. Because the nervous system had to overcome the resistance of the athlete's body weight plus gravity, it recruited more muscles for the last jump. The use of more muscles should translate into more height on the final jump. Aerobic training, on the other hand, essentially requires having the body engage in activities (e.g., running, swimming, etc.) in which the major muscles of the body are engaged for an extended period of time on a non-stop basis.

As strange as it may seem, softball pitchers need jumping power. Every single pitch is a function of power. All factors considered, the more muscles the nerves can recruit to throw the ball, the stronger the delivery of the ball will be.

SAMPLE STRENGTHENING PROGRAM

The sample program explained in this chapter is designed for players of all ages. It is designed to improve a pitcher's strength, power, coordination, agility, and flexibility. An athlete who has never lifted weights before or has not lifted weights in the past several months should start with the beginner-level program. This program is the foundation on which she should continue to build. The athlete should not move onto the next phase until she is able to complete the listed sets and repetitions for all of the exercises. An athlete should consult a strength and conditioning specialist or a qualified coach about the correct form of the exercises if she decides to do them on her own. To help prevent injuries, she should be sure to warm up and cool down properly before and after each work out.

AEROBIC FITNESS

The second component of a complete fitness program is aerobic conditioning. Aerobic conditioning involves training the body's metabolic (energy) pathways. Basic aerobic conditioning addresses two types of training—without oxygen (anaerobic) and with oxygen (aerobic). Anaerobic training traditionally involves some sprint-type work. While anaerobic conditioning is the primary focus for softball players, a pitcher also needs to be aerobically fit. Pitchers may work on aerobic conditioning using a variety of activities, including running, biking, working on a mechanical stair climbing machine, working on a ski machine, rowing, swimming, and aerobic dance classes. An athlete who is just initiating an aerobic fitness program should start with 20- to 25-minute sessions, four to five days a week. After two to three weeks, the athlete should increase her workouts to 30- to 40-minute sessions, five to six days a week. This aerobic work should continue for six to eight weeks, at which point, the pitcher should then switch to anaerobic conditioning. For anaerobic conditioning, the activities should be of shorter duration (10 minutes or less per activity) and higher intensity. For example, if the pitcher is riding a stationary bike, she should pedal at either a higher level of resistance or a higher RPM for five to 10 minutes, decrease the resistance or speed for five minutes, then repeat the higher pace or resistance.

HOW TO MONITOR AEROBIC OR ANAEROBIC EXERCISE

Heart rate and total exercise time determine what energy source (anaerobic or aerobic) is used during a particular exercise segment. The point to remember is that if an athlete is training her aerobic system, she should be able to hold a conversation with a partner during the activity. While conversation should be slightly difficult to conduct, she should not be totally out of breath. The exercise bout should last 15 to 40 minutes, depending on the athlete's fitness level.

On the other hand, when conditioning her anaerobic system, an athlete should not be able to hold a conversation with her partner. She should be breathing heavily, indicating that her heart rate is high. This pace will be hard, if not impossible, to sustain for a long period of time (over two minutes continuously), which is why the athlete who is attempting to develop her anaerobic fitness level should exercise hard for a short period of time, rest for a period of time, and then repeat the exercise.

WARMING UP AND COOLING DOWN

Warming up, cooling down, and stretching should also be vital components of an athlete's physical workout routine. Her warm-up should be a less intense version of the activity the athlete is preparing to do. If she will be lifting weights, she should do warm-up exercises that concentrate on the muscles she will be using. The cool-down should also mimic the workout. Stretching should involve dynamic movements to warm up and static movements to cool down. The program presented in this chapter includes warm-up and cool-down exercises. When conditioning, an athlete should include approximately five minutes before the primary workout to warm up and approximately five minutes afterwards to cool down.

Strength Training: Phase I (Beginner)

	Phase 1	Phase 2	Phase 3
Skips	4 x 20 yards	4 x 25 yards	4 x 25 yards
Lateral Line Hops	4 x 20 seconds	4 x 25 seconds	4 x 25 seconds
Body Weight Squats	4 x 15	4 x 25	4 x 35
Push-Ups	10	15	20
Back Arcs	3 x 12	3 x 15	3 x 20
Crunches	3 x 12	3 x 20	3 x 30
Hip Abduction	2 x 15	2 x 20	2 x 30
Curl-Ups	2 x 12	3 x 15	3 x 20
Mountain Climbers	3 x 12	3 x 30	3 x 40
Single Leg Squats	1 x 10	1 x 15	1 x 20
Shoulder Routine	1 x 12	1 x 15	1 x 20
Wrist Curls (5 lbs.)	1 x failure	2 x failure	3 x failure

Strength Training: Phase II (Intermediate)

	Phase 1	Phase 2	Phase 3
Split Jumps	4 x 20 seconds	4 x 25 seconds	4 x 25 seconds
Squat Jumps	3 x 15 seconds	3 x 20 seconds	3 x 20 seconds
Cone/Object Jumps	10	15	20
Dumbbell Squats	3 x 12	3 x 15	3 x 20
Push-Ups	25	25	30
Back Arcs	2 x 15	2 x 20	2 x 30
Curl-Ups	2 x 12	3 x 15	3 x 20
Lunges	3 x 12	3 x 20	3 x 25
Tuck-Ups	2 x 10	2 x 15	2 x 20
Shoulder Routine	1 x 12	1 x 15	1 x 20
Wrist Curls (15 lbs.)	1 x failure	2 x failure	3 x failure

Strength Training: Phase II (Advanced)

	Phase 1	Phase 2	Phase 3
Tuck Jumps	3 x 15	3 x 20	3 x 20
Lateral Box Jumps	10	15	20
Squat Jumps	3 x 12	3 x 15	3 x 20
Squats-Bar	4 x 8	4 x 10	4 x 10
Push-Ups	2 x 15	2 x 20	2 x 30
Step-Ups	2 x 12	3 x 15	3 x 20
Back Arcs-Leg Curl	3 x 12	3 x 20	3 x 25
Walking Lunge	2 x 10	2 x 15	2 x 20
Shoulder Routine	1 x 12	1 x 15	1 x 20
Wrist Curls (25 lbs.)	1 x failure	2 x failure	3 x failure

Diagram 6-1: Pushup—starting position

Diagram 6-2: Pushup—mid-range exercise position

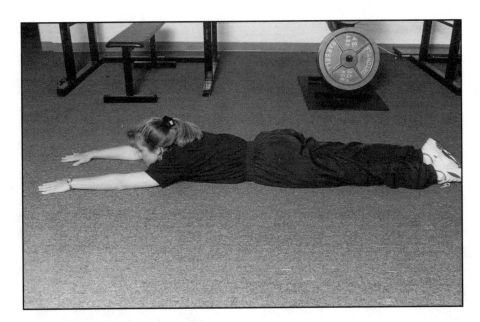

Diagram 6-3: Back arc—starting position

Diagram 6-4: Back arc—mid-range exercise position

Diagram 6-5: Dumbbell squat—starting position

Diagram 6-6: Dumbbell squat—mid-range exercise position

Diagram 6-7: Squat jump—starting position

Diagram 6-8: Squat jump—mid-range exercise position

Diagram 6-9: Step-up (body weight)—initial movement

Diagram 6-10: Step-up (body weight)—mid-range exercise position

Diagram 6-11: Step-up (dumbbell)—initial movement

Diagram 6-12: Step-up (dumbbell)—mid-range exercise position

Diagram 6-13: Shoulder shrug—starting position

Diagram 6-14: Shoulder shrug—mid-range exercise position

Diagram 6-15: External Rotation—starting position

Diagram 6-16: External rotation: mid-range exercise position

Diagram 6-17: Wrist curls—starting position

Diagram 6-18: Wrist curls—mid-range exercise position

Diagram 6-19: Walking lunge—mid-range exercise position

STRETCHING EXERCISES

An athlete's muscles are designed to be long, flexible and lean. As such, the ability of each of the skeletal joints in the body (over 100) to move through its natural range of motion is determined by the inherent elasticity of the surrounding musculature and connective tissue. The best way to maintain that elasticity is by stretching. Stretching exercises are designed to require muscles to move through their full range of motion. Accordingly, an athlete who stretches properly will be better prepared to perform at an optimal level and less likely to suffer a musculo-skeletal joint injury.

V-Stretch

The player should sit with her back straight and her legs extended in the shape of a V. She should wrap a rope or towel around the middle of her foot. Using the rope or towel, she should slowly pull her upper torso down toward her foot. Once the stretch is felt in her hamstring, she should stop and hold the stretch for three seconds, then relax. The stretch should be repeated three to five times per leg.

Diagram 6-20: V-stretch

Glutes and Hip Stretch
Glutes, Hip Rotators

The player should place the right ankle on top of the left knee. She should the grasp behind the left knee with both hands and pull the knee toward her chest until a stretch is felt in the right buttocks, and then hold for five seconds. She should repeat the stretch three times per leg.

Diagram 6-21: Glutes and hip stretch

Low Back Stretch

The player should sit with a slight bend in her knees. Keeping her feet apart, she should grasp both feet and pull until a stretch is felt in the hamstrings and/or lower back.

Diagram 6-22: Low back stretch

Rotary Torso

The player should keep her head and hips in line with each other. She should have the bat threaded through her arms behind her back. She should rotate her shoulders to the right, hold for five seconds, rotate back to center, rotate to the left, hold for five seconds, and repeat.

Diagram 6-23: Rotary torso stretch

Diagram 6-24: Hamstring stretch

Hamstring Stretch

With a straight back and slightly bent knees, the player should bend slowly at the hips until a stretch is felt in her hamstrings.

Side Stretch

The player should hold the bat overhead in both hands. She should then pull the bat to one side. After holding the stretch for five seconds, she should then repeat on the other side.

Diagram 6-25: Side stretch

Chest Stretch

The player should hold the bat overhead with both hands. She should pull the bat back behind her head until she feels the stretch in her chest and shoulders.

Diagram 6-26: Chest stretch

Quad Stretch

The player should lie on her left side, propped up on her left forearm. She should grasp her right ankle with her right hand and pull her leg back until she feels the stretch in her quadricep, hold the stretch for three seconds, and then relax. She should repeat the stretch three times, then roll onto her right side, and repeat the stretch for her left leg.

**Diagram 6-27:
Quad stretch**

Butterfly Stretch

The player should sit up straight, place the soles of her feet together, and pull them into her body. Grasping both feet, she should pull the torso down toward the feet until the stretch is felt in the inner thigh (adductor) and/or lower back (spinal erector). She should hold the stretch for five seconds, relax, and repeat three times.

**Diagram 6-28:
Butterfly
stretch**

IN-SEASON AND OUT-OF-SEASON PITCHING WORKOUTS

Many different schools of thought exist regarding the number of pitches a pitcher should throw and the number of days per week she should work out in-season and out-of-season. It is the coach's responsibility to acknowledge that each pitcher is unique and, as such, should be handled accordingly. Focusing on the quality of pitches thrown is much more beneficial than focusing on the quantity of pitches thrown. Over-throwing or throwing too much when tired causes a pitcher to practice bad habits. Since pitchers tend to play like they practice, practicing bad habits will only cause problems in games.

Because all pitchers are different and have different needs, there is no one "right" workout. There is also no "right" or "wrong" number of pitches to throw. Some pitchers like to work out hard two or three days a week during the season and rest the day before a game, then work out four to five days a week during the off-season. Other pitchers prefer to work out one or two days a week during the season, throw the day before a game, and work out six days a week during the off-season. Some pitchers can be warmed up for a game in 20 minutes; others require an hour. The coach and her pitchers should find out what works best for each individual to help that athlete maximize her level of improvement.

Before choosing a workout, it is important to determine whether a pitcher is at the beginner, intermediate, or advanced level. Age, size, shape, and athletic ability do not necessarily determine that level. A beginning pitcher can be an eight-year-old playing ball for the first time or a 20-year-old whose team needs another pitcher. A beginner is usually defined as a pitcher who is still working on the basic fundamentals of her delivery, especially balance. A beginner may be able to throw two pitches, the fastball and the change-up, but is probably still working on her delivery style and her ability to hit locations.

The intermediate level is a harder category to define because many pitchers who belong at the intermediate level see themselves as advanced. A pitcher is at the intermediate level when she possesses three or four pitches (e.g., rise ball, drop ball, change-up, and possibly a curve ball) and is still working on the ability to put the correct movement on the ball and to hit locations with those pitches at the same time.

At the advanced level, a pitcher usually has a full repertoire of pitches (e.g., rise ball, drop ball, curve ball, screwball, change-up, and several variations). An advanced pitcher is developed by several years of intense pitching workouts and game experience. A coach should compare her pitcher to the top collegiate pitchers (the advanced level) to help determine exactly into which category she falls.

PITCHING WORKOUT: BEGINNER LEVEL

The following workout is designed to work on a pitcher's balance and location and increase her leg drive. It should be performed for approximately a week. The coach can add or delete drills to tailor it to each pitcher. After she has warmed up, a beginning pitcher should not throw intensely for more than 30 to 40 minutes.

- Throw 10-15 balls from second base to home in the air without an arc (works on leg drive).
- Throw 10-15 balls from about 15 feet with no step (checks balance and body position).
- Go through 10-20 Phase I freeze drills (check foot placement and balance).
- Throw 10-15 fastballs and make sure the pitcher is completely warmed up.
- Throw 5-10 inside fastballs and 5-10 outside fastballs, then alternate for 10-20 pitches.
- Always end on a good pitch.

PITCHING WORKOUT: INTERMEDIATE LEVEL

The following workout, for an intermediate player, is designed to work on leg drive; a good, quick wrist snap; location; and switching from one pitch to another. This workout should be conducted over an approximately one-week period, focusing on a different pitch each time it is performed.

- Throw 10-15 pitches from second.
- Throw 10-15 walk-throughs back to the mound.
- Throw 15-20 pitches with a good wrist snap and no step.
- Throw 10-15 final pitches to complete warm-up.
- Throw 10-15 inside drop balls.
- Throw 10-15 outside drop balls.
- Throw six sets of alternating inside and outside drop balls (one set is two to each side, or four pitches).
- Throw 5-10 change-ups.
- Throw 3 sets of alternating drop balls and change-ups to different locations.

PITCHING WORKOUT: ADVANCED LEVEL

The following program provides a sample workout for the advanced pitcher. It is designed to work on leg drive; quick, strong wrist snaps; fine-tuning the drop ball and rise ball; switching between two different pitches; and physical and mental practice of a possible inning. When working on two different pitches, it is helpful to choose two pitches that require the body to do completely different things, such as the drop ball and rise ball.

- Throw 15+ long-distance pitches from second base or centerfield.
- Throw 10 walk-throughs back to the mound.
- Throw 10 pitches with good wrist snaps from close range.
- Throw 10+ good rise balls, alternating inside and outside.
- Throw 10+ good drop balls, alternating inside and outside.
- Throw five sets of mixed rise balls and drop balls to various locations.

Diagram 6-29: Training to become a successful pitcher involves more than just throwing "x" number of pitches and learning "x" number of new pitches.

CHAPTER 7

Zeroing in on the Hitters

A pitcher who observes and responds appropriately to all the information given to her by a hitter will enhance the likelihood that she will be successful. For example, body language says a lot about a hitter. From the moment a hitter steps into the on-deck circle, she begins to send out messages that either the catcher or the coach should look for, such as signs of distraction, lack of concentration, nervousness, or frustration. A pitcher should not be distracted from the hitter at the plate by the player in the on-deck circle, but any information that can be gathered from the batter may help keep the pitcher ahead of the game.

As a hitter approaches the box, she is typically receiving signals from her coach, looking at where the defense is playing, and sometimes even looking at the pitcher. All factors considered, pitchers can be encouraged to make direct eye contact with the batter. After all the pitcher should appear dominant and in charge. The coach can help teach a pitcher to be confident and in charge with body language.

As a rule, a hitter's stance will give the pitcher and her catcher information that can be utilized immediately. The pitcher and catcher often face the same batter several times during the course of a game. Once they have faced a batter, they should have a "history" on that batter that can provide them with a great deal of useful information.

If it is the first time a pitcher has faced a particular hitter, she should make several observations and ask herself a few questions relating to these "discoveries." The catcher should also be required to closely observe the hitter to relieve the pitcher of some of the responsibility in this regard in order to enable the pitcher to focus more on the pitching process. In cases where she does not have an experienced catcher, the pitcher should be able to identify a hitter's weaknesses on her own.

The point to be emphasized is that pitchers should get used to asking themselves several questions before they throw a pitch. While beginning pitchers may feel a little overwhelmed trying to gather this information, asking these questions and making quick observations will help pave the pitchers' road to success. Among the questions that should be asked before throwing the first pitch to a batter are the following:

- Is the batter standing up or back in the box?
- Is she crowding the plate or away from the plate?
- Where are her hands—high, low, or tight?
- Is her stance open or closed?

After the first swing, the pitcher should reevaluate the situation and ask herself several additional questions, including:

- Did the batter swing long or sweep at the ball?
- Did she over-stride?
- Did she have a hitch in her swing?
- Did she shy away from the pitch or did she want the pitch?

The point to keep in mind is that pitching involves a lot more than just throwing the ball. The better a pitcher gets at identifying a batter's strengths and weaknesses, the better she will be at understanding when and why she should throw a particular pitch. A coach can help by standing in as a batter with different stances so the pitchers can practice picking up a batter's unique signals. This is also a great rainy day workout. The coach may also present the pitchers with different scenarios and see what pitch they would throw in a particular situation. Among the questions a coach might ask her pitchers are the following:

- A runner is at first; no outs; and the batter's stance is open and at the front of the box. What is the situation? What should the pitcher throw?
- The batter has a closed stance and her hands are very high. What should the pitcher throw? What red flags does she see?
- The batter is crowding the plate and has low, tight hands. What should the pitcher throw? What red flags does she see?
- The batter swung at the first pitch and has a long stride toward third. What should the pitcher throw? What red flags does she see?
- The bases are loaded in the seventh inning; one out; the pitcher's team is up by one run; and the batter has tight hands. What is the situation? What should the pitcher throw?

While no absolutes exist in the game of softball, most of the time hitters will tend to allow the pitcher to set them up. Accordingly, the pitcher should always be thinking and observing the hitters and the situation. To the extent possible, she should use any information available to her to her advantage.

CHAPTER 8

Homework in Pitching

Homework is an essential prerequisite for a pitcher. In fact, many coaches believe that properly done homework can change the outcome of over 50 percent of the games played. Accordingly, because of its potential to make a significant difference in a game, every pitcher must address the issue of homework.

A pitcher should always put herself in position to succeed. Part of doing that is gathering all the information available on the batters from the team she is about to face. Pitching charts can work for every pitcher, regardless of her ability or repertoire of pitches.

Several different types of pitching charts are available to be used by players and coaches. No single chart is correct; it is really a matter of personal preference. The pitcher and the catcher should be comfortable with the charts that they decide to employ since they are the ones who will be using all the information the charts can provide.

Pitching charts typically provide a substantial amount of very useful information concerning a particular hitter, including what pitches a batter swung at, what pitches she didn't want, what she did during each at bat, and where she tends to hit the ball. A pitching chart tells a pitcher what worked against that batter and what has not worked. Charts A and B provide two examples of pitching charts that can be used to compile and stockpile a batter's history and vital information. The point to remember is that, all factors considered, the more details provided on these charts, the better off the pitcher will be. Another player (preferably a pitcher or a catcher) who is not on defense should keep the charts so the coach is free to work and watch her team.

Date: _____
Lady Razorbacks vs _____

Pitcher: _____ **Notes:** _____
Catcher: _____ _____
_____
_____

Score: _____
_____

#_ _	#_ _	#_ _
#_ _	#_ _	#_ _
#_ _	#_ _	#_ _

Diagram 8-1: A sample pitching chart (Chart A)

Chart A shows home plate. This type of pitching chart is generally used to record the following information:

- The hitter's name and jersey number.
- Whether she is right-handed or left-handed or a switch hitter.
- Where she stands in the box.
- Whether she has an open or closed stance.
- What she did with previous at-bats.
- As many details as possible.

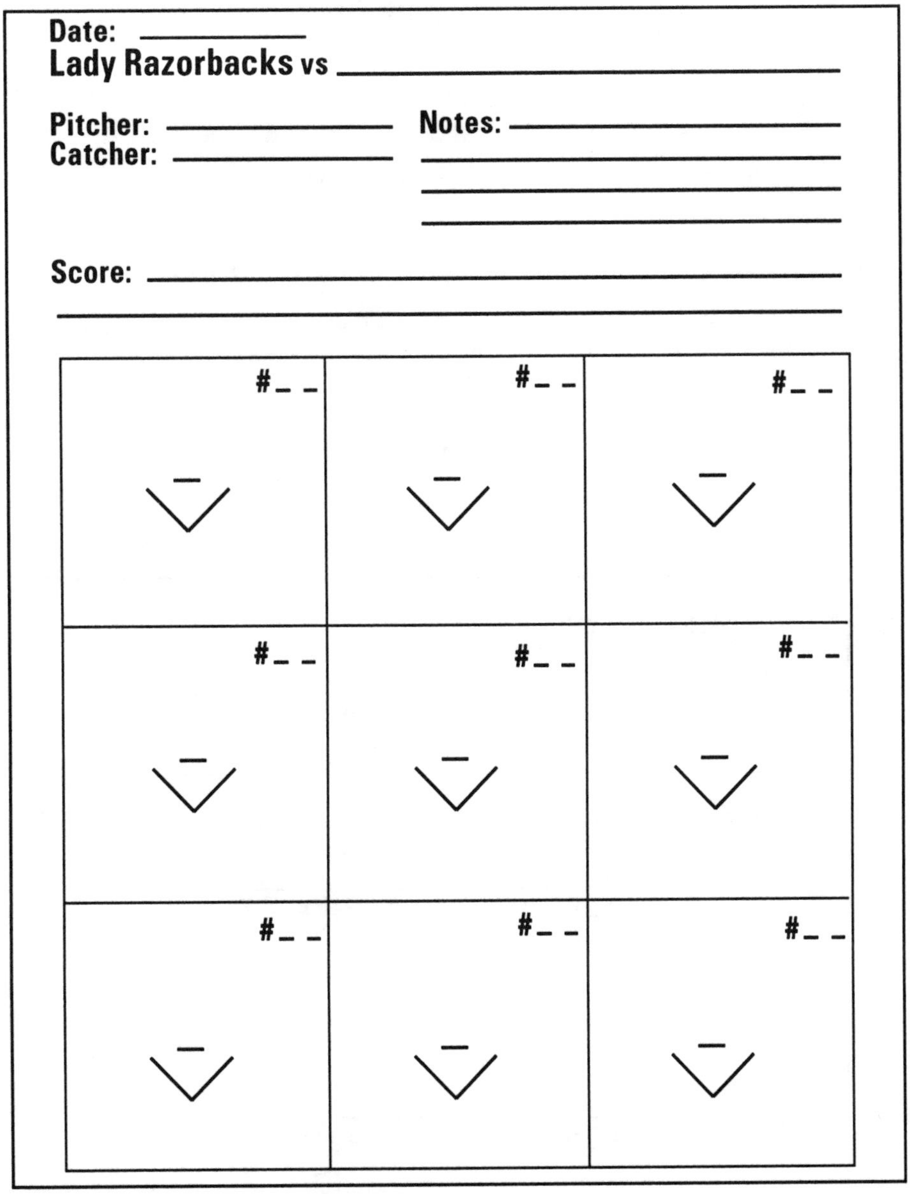

Diagram 8-2: A sample pitching chart (Chart B)

Chart B shows a small field. This type of pitching chart is used to record the following additional information:

- The hitter's jersey number.
- What pitches the pitcher threw.
- What the batter did with each pitch.
- What the defense did on each play.
- As many details as possible.

Examples of partially completed Charts A and B are illustrated in Diagrams 8-3 and 8-4, respectively. It is important to use abbreviations for noting information and details on the charts that the pitcher and catcher are both comfortable and familiar with. For example, the following abbreviations can be used in the Chart A.

- TH = tight hands
- OS = open hands
- UP = up in box
- BK = back in box
- C = hits change
- PH = pull hitter
- FS = free swinger

- L = lunges
- HM = hand movement
- CC = can't hit change
- CS = closed stance
- SA = steps away
- SI = steps in
- H = Hitch

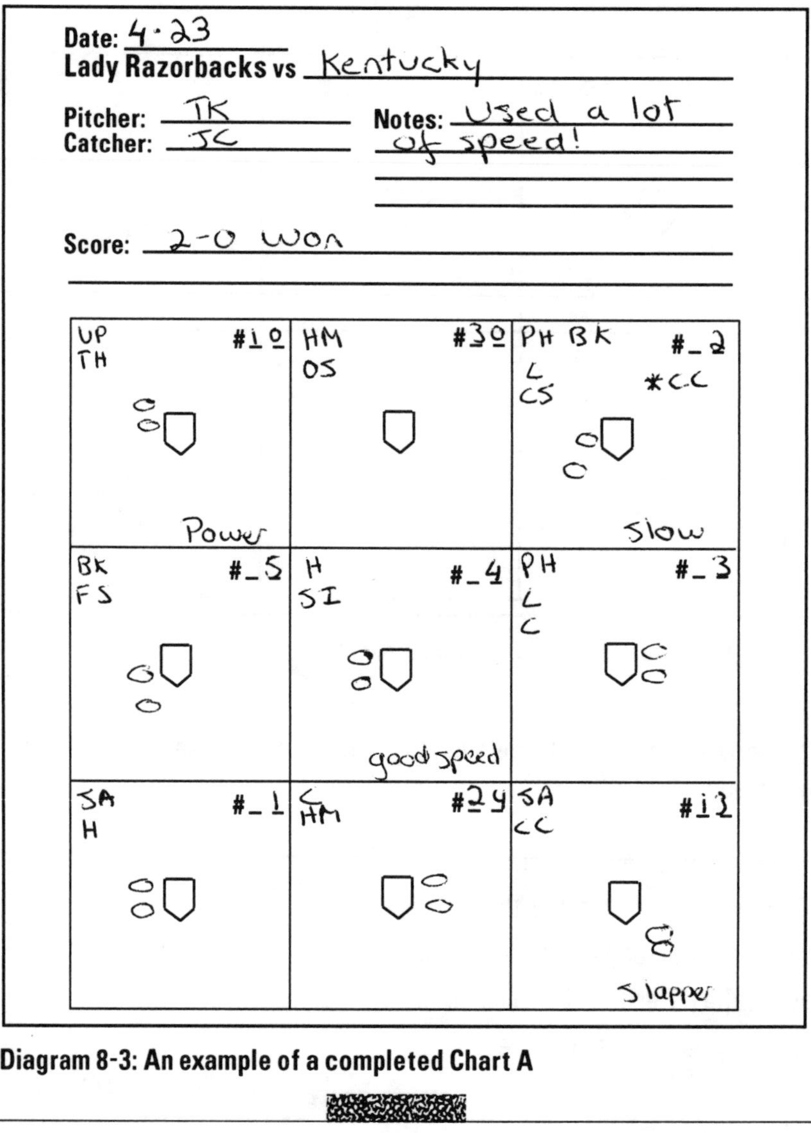

Diagram 8-3: An example of a completed Chart A

The following abbreviations can be utilized with Chart B:

- B = ball
- BB = base on balls
- LD = line drive
- F = fly the ball with position
- FB = foul ball
- CS = called strike
- HB = hit batter
- GB = ground ball

- K = strike out
- SS = swinging strike
- Ʞ = looking strike out
- 1B = Base Hit
- 2B = Double
- 3B = Triple
- HR = HR

Four type of pitch first number:

* 1 = rise   * 2 = drop
* 3 = curve   * 4 = screw
* 5 = change

For location of pitch second number:

* 1 = left shoulder of catcher
* 2 = left knee of catcher
* 3 = right knee of catcher
*4 = right shoulder of catcher

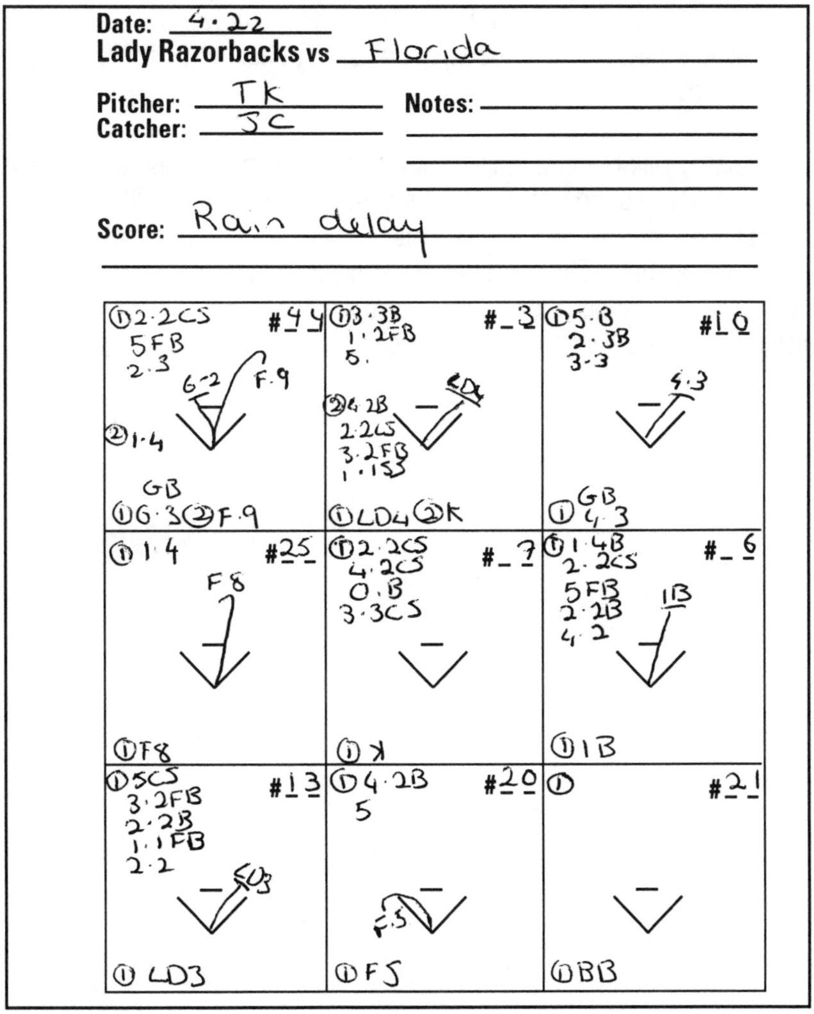

Date: 4·22

Lady Razorbacks vs Florida

Pitcher: Tk   **Notes:** _____

Catcher: JC

Score: Rain delay

①2·2CS #4 4 5FB 2·3 6·2 F·9 ②1·4 GB ①6·3②F·9	③·3B #_3 1·2FB 5· ④4·2B 2·2CS 3·2FB 1·1SS ①LD4②K	①5·B #_LO 2·3B 3·3 5·3 GB ①4·3
①1·4 #25 F8 ①F8	①2·2CS #_7 4·2CS 0·B 3·3CS ① Ʞ	①1·4B #_6 2·2CS 5FB 13 2·2B 4·2 ①1B
①5CS #13 3·2FB 2·2B 1·1FB 2·2 ①LD3	①4·2B #20 5 ①FJ	① #21 ①BB

Diagram 8-4: An example of a completed Chart B

It can be very helpful to use both charts together. Chart A is used to record the hitter's physical characteristics and any important information about her. Chart B is used to keep track of every pitch thrown and what happened with each pitch.

If possible, a pitcher should know who she will face and what her game plan will be prior to the game. A tournament provides even more opportunities to gather information than regular season games. The pitcher and catcher should watch the upcoming opponent play another team and chart the hitters. This observation can help boost the pitcher's confidence and enable her to get a grasp of the opposing hitters' tendencies. It is also a great time to watch a hitter's body language and practice picking up all the signals and cues that a hitter typically sends out.

Besides all the homework the pitcher can do to prepare before the game—a lot of discussion and preparation should also take place between innings between a pitcher and her catcher. Both of these key players should literally love sharing the knowledge that they gain from their on-going observations with each other. If a pitcher works closely with her catcher and does her homework, she will take the field with the attitude that the opponents must beat her. In the process, her game may be raised to new level.

The coach should talk to her pitcher about what she can do to increase the odds in her favor. As a rule, a good hitter will hit somewhere between .300 and .400 at the elite college level. In other words, even the best hitters only get three to four hits out of every ten at-bats. That statistic alone gives the pitcher a sixty- to seventy-percent chance of success. If a pitcher has done her homework, she may be able to eliminate one of those hits, thereby increasing her chances of success even more.

CHAPTER 9

Using the Information

At this point, the pitcher should be able to put together everything she has learned, even if she has not yet mastered all of the different pitches. If her goal is to reach the elite level, she must master both movement and location for all of her pitches. Pitching greats like Joan Joyce or Barb Renaldi did not necessarily have the best rise ball or drop ball; their key to success was their ability to hit any location with the pitch. Similarly, the 1996 Chinese Olympic team did not throw the ball particularly hard or have great ball movement, but they were very successful because each of their pitches was almost always where the catcher called for it.

An important point of emphasis is to remember that one of the cardinal sins in pitching is missing both movement and location. A pitcher will often escape unharmed if she misses one, but missing both usually leads to trouble.

A quick reference for the beginning pitcher is the release point—that box right at the hip. If she is throwing the ball high, she is releasing out in front of that box. If she is throwing the ball low or bouncing it to the plate, then she is releasing the ball before she reaches the box. If the ball is going outside, she is coming across her body outside of that box, and if the ball is going inside, her release is pulling away from her body outside the box.

Different game situations call for different pitches. Chart 9-1 lists specific game situations, what pitch would be good to throw in those situations, and why. The coach should remember that these guidelines are not absolutes; a pitcher may make a different choice based on how good her specific pitch is, the history and tendencies of the batter she is facing, and her level of confidence.

Game Situation	What Pitch	Reason
Bunt	Rise ball, screw ball	The batter will go up or move her arms to the ball, meaning there is a good chance the batter will pop the bunt up.
Run-n-Slap	Outside drop ball, screw ball, change-up	The batter tends to pull or take her first step away from the ball. Since the batter is already in motion, a change of speed will make the batter early on the pitch.
Slap that steps towards plate	Inside rise, inside drop, curve	The batter is trying to go to the left side of the field, the inside pitch makes it harder
Fly ball to left side	Inside rise ball or screw ball to a right-handed batter, outside rise ball to a left-handed batter	The rise ball makes batters tend to fly out; the screw ball keeps the ball on the correct side of the plate to get the batter to hit to the right side whether they hit from the left to the right side.
Fly ball to right side	Outside rise ball or curve ball to right-handed batters, inside rise ball to left-handed batters	The rise ball makes batters tend to fly out; the curve ball keeps the ball on the correct side of the plate to get the batter to hit to the right side whether they hit from the left or the right side.
Ground ball to right side	Outside drop ball, low outside change-up, curve ball to right-handed batters. All the same pitches to a left-handed batter thrown inside	Batters tend to hit drop balls down into the ground. The batter will be out in front with the off speed pitch and only use her arms; the curve ball will take the ball to the right side with both hitters.

Chart 9-1: A pitcher's guide to specific game situations

Game Situation	What Pitch	Reason
Ground ball to left side	Inside drop ball, low inside change, low inside curve ball to right-handed batters. Inside low screw ball, outside drop ball outside low change-up to left-handed batters	Batters tend to hit drop balls down into the ground. On the off-speed pitch, the batter will be out in front and pull the ball to the left side; the curve ball and screw ball will take the ball to the left side.
Bases Loaded	Drop ball to either side, low curve ball to either side	If there are less than two outs, the drop ball should be thrown to keep the ball on the ground. If there are two outs, a fly ball or ground ball will work.
Runner in scoring position	Right-handed hitter: drop ball inside, curve ball inside, change-up low inside, screw ball. Left-handed hitter: screw ball, outside drop ball, outside curve ball.	The ball will be hit on the ground to the left side of the infield. This situation should keep the runner at second even if the ball is not fielded cleanly.
Strike out pitch	The pitcher's "bread and butter" pitch	Chart 9-2 is designed to use a hitters' weaknesses and tendencies to help select a pitch that will be effective against that hitter.

Chart 9-1 (cont.): A pitcher's guide to specific game situations

Pitch	When to Throw	Why
Rise ball	• Batter up in box • Inside tight hands • Long stride • Batter crowds plate	• Moves through swing • Cannot get hands on top of ball • Eyes and body move through stride zone
Drop ball	• Hands high • Bails out with stride • Run-n-slap batter whose first step is to first • Pitcher wants to keep the ball in the infield	• Can't get to ball • Hard to hit with power • Hard to lift
Curve ball	• Crowds plate (inside curve) • Steps into plate (inside curve) • Lunges at ball • Stands far away from plate • Steps away from plate	• Makes weight transfer break • Batter is hitting only with her arms and has no power • Batter can't cover plate
Screw ball	• Strides into plate • Sweeping swing • Slapper who pulls or steps to first • Hitter trying to hit to the right side • Opposite field hitter	• Breaks into knee area and takes away power • Breaks away from a slapper so all she can do is lunge
Change-up	• Great all the time • Early on ball • Hand movement • Overstriding • Pulling ball	• Timing off • Breaks the speed • Batter is hitting only with her arms and has no power

Chart 9-2: A pitcher's guide to specific pitches

Beyond game situations and batters' tendencies, every pitcher has a "bread-and-butter" pitch. This pitch is the pitch she is always able to throw well—the pitch that always seems to work. This is the pitch the pitcher will throw in difficult situations or when she has to throw a strike. There is a lot that can be said for the "bread-and-butter" pitch and the confidence a pitcher has in it. Sometimes a pitcher's instinct is the best indicator of which pitch to throw, regardless of what the game situation would seem to dictate.

THE WEATHER

Softball is an outdoor sport and many players have played in snow, rain, and wind. Heat can also be a factor, although the sun should not be. In wet weather, it is harder to grip the ball, and the pitches do not always move as much as they should. In extremely cold weather, all the athletes tend to perform more slowly, including the pitcher and the hitter. The pitcher should do her best to stay warm during and between innings. Wind can work either for or against a pitcher, depending on which way it is blowing. Pitching into the wind can be good for throwing a knuckleball and its movement. It should be noted, however, that such a situation will tend to slow the ball down a little. Throwing into the wind also means the ball will be hit farther. Throwing with the wind can aid the pitcher by increasing the speed and movement of the ball on all her pitches.

THE MENTAL GAME

History and homework can elevate a pitcher's game to a whole new level. The point that should be emphasized is that she should use all of the tools at her disposal to get into the best part of pitching—the mental game.

CHAPTER 10

Problem Solving

Although every pitcher would like to pitch perfectly, it is important for her and her coach to know where to start when trying to solve problems that may arise with her pitching. Whether a pitcher is at the beginner, intermediate, or advanced level, trouble shooting can begin in one of three areas: the components of a pitch, the location of the ball, or the specific pitch.

THE COMPONENTS OF PITCH

Chart 10-1 addresses the same basic breakdown of a successful pitch that was discussed earlier. Chart 10-1 is broken down into four primary elements: the specific area of concentration; the problem; the outcome of the problem; and the potential solutions to a particular problem.

Area of Concentration	Problem	Outcome	Solution
Grip	White knuckles	High location; slower speed; cannot attain a spin	Have pitcher grip the ball as hard as possible and throw overhand. Compare to gripping a bat with white knuckles.
	No air pocket (like palm ball)	Slow speed; pushing ball	Put ball onto fingertips.
	Not using seam	Loose ball; can't see rotation; less spin	Have pitcher put fingertips on seams and feel the security it will provide.

Chart 10-1: Evaluating problems involving components of pitch

Area of Concentration	Problem	Outcome	Solution
Foot Placement	Feet too close together	Lack of balance; not capable of maximizing drive; slower speed	Keep feet shoulder width apart.
	Not using rubber or mound to drive	Slower pitch; hard to advance to other pitches	Have foot rock from heel to toe to feel the push, then look for the push-off hole and the drag mark.
The Dance	Bend at waist	Pitch thrown with arm; lack of leg drive	Practice walk-through drill. Have pitcher drive with shoulders slightly back.
	Jerky motion	Doesn't maximize speed or fluid; quick release	Have pitcher throw a relaxed pitch from a longer distance (not for speed, but to cover ground). Videotape the pitcher to give her a visual aid. Videotape a jerky bat swing for comparison.
	Cloning	Lack of rhythm; never find comfort zone	Have pitchers try several motions to find their own dance.
Balance	Falling or driving toward glove arm	Hips never fully rotate open; pitcher will tend to throw with her shoulder.	Practice Phase I drill, wall drill, and one knee drill.
	Weight over stride foot	Timing off; throwing with arm instead of legs; throws release point off	Practice Phase I drill. Have the pitcher concentrate on feeling the weight transfer and push off.

Chart 10-1 (cont.): Evaluating problems involving the components of a pitch

Area of Concentration	Problem	Outcome	Solution
Balance cont.	Weight left on push-off foot	No power; ball will be high in zone	Practice Phase I drill; then throw through to Phase II to focus on the weight transfer and when it takes place.
	Dipping to throw with arm	Pitcher throws only with her arm; ball is released high (outside of the box)	Hold the pitcher's glove shoulder through the release. Practice mirror drill.
Weight Transfer	All weight transferred to stride leg on foot plant	No power; throwing 90% with arm while off-balance	Have pitcher throw to feel the weight transfer and when it is taking place. Videotape pitcher from the side so she can see the incorrect weight transfer.
	Shift of weight	Drive is not to target but to the glove side of the body; hard to keep weight on push-off foot for power	Rock from foot to foot to imitate drive.
	Transfer up/ forward	Lack of power; more of a step instead of a drive	Have pitcher sprint to feel lateral power, then jump to feel vertical power so she can feel the difference.
Hip Rotation	Hips that stay open	Ball tends to go to the right side of the plate	Have pitcher throw with no step to feel how she can rotate hips. Practice mirror drill.
	Hips that never open	Foot plant will be at 12 o'clock; pitcher is left with no power; release point is shortened	Have pitcher set up in Phase I, then put her plant foot between one and two o'clock on the power line.

Chart 10-1 (cont.): Evaluating problems involving the components of a pitch

Area of Concentration	Problem	Outcome	Solution
Drive	Lazy	No power; very little distance will be covered	Compare to the result of a lazy bat swing.
Stride and Foot Plant	Short	No power; bad weight transfer; no rhythm	Draw a line in the dirt that the pitcher must clear with her stride foot. Push from the small of her back and force her to drive so she can feel the difference.
	Long	Weight transfer is off balance; throw is with the arm only; can lead to crow hopping or dipping of the shoulder	Put a glove or tape on the ground and do not allow the pitcher to stride past that spot. Have pitcher get in Phase I and put her stride foot on the power line at the proper distance.
	Too close to ground	Does not allow maximum power	Put a small object on the ground that the pitcher must clear with her stride foot.
	Too high	Takes power vertically instead of laterally	Practice mirror drill and cement drill.
	12 o'clock	Never allows proper hip rotation to occur	Break pitch down into Phase I and Phase II, stressing the power line.
	3 o'clock	Hard on stride knee; leaves hips open at the release	Break pitch down into Phase I and Phase II, stressing the power line.

Chart 10-1 (cont.): Evaluating problems involving the components of a pitch

Area of Concentration	Problem	Outcome	Solution
Release	Slow or Lazy	Ball stays on hand too long; slowing the speed	Work on a quick, flicking release. Practice big-ball spin drill.
Follow Through	Not ready for defense	Opens up for an offensive attack and makes the defense weak	Practice follow-through drill. The pitcher should believe she is an essential component of the defense. Practice ground balls and bunts.

Chart 10-1 (cont.): Evaluating problems involving the components of pitch

THE LOCATION OF THE PITCH

Another major issue that must be addressed (from a problem-solving standpoint) is the location of the pitch, regardless of the type of pitch thrown. A pitcher has a very small box from which she must release the ball in order to throw a strike. This box is roughly six to eight inches in length and five to seven inches in width. The size of the box, however, can vary based on different pitching distances and size of the pitcher.

If a pitch is too high, the ball is being released in front of the release box. Likewise, if the pitch is too low or bounces before reaching the plate, the ball is being released behind the box. If a right-hander's pitch is to the outside of the plate against a right-handed hitter (or to the inside from a left-handed pitcher), she is going across her leg, or out to the left of the box, during her release. If a pitcher is throwing the ball to the inside of the plate, her arm is out away from her body and out to the right of the box.

An improper release point is not the only reason a pitch is high, low, inside, or outside. Many other factors can also affect the location of the pitch, including the pitcher bending at the waist, or dipping her shoulders, the pitcher incorrectly planting her stride or foot plant, or the pitcher throwing a ball that lacks rotation.

The important thing to remember when dealing with location is to always make the appropriate adjustment. If a pitcher throws a ball high twice, the third pitch may bounce, but it should never go high. This action lets the coach know the pitcher is making an adjustment to her release. If a pitcher continues to struggle with her location, however, a good possibility exists that another problem is affecting her pitch.

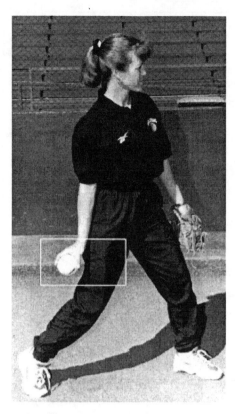

Diagram 10-1: A pitcher has a very small box from which she must release the ball in order to throw a strike.

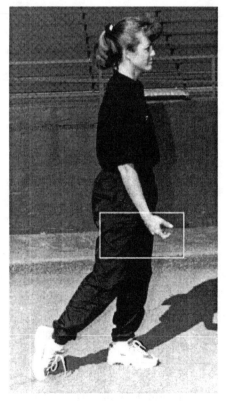

Diagram 10-2: The size of the box can vary, based on different pitching distances and the size of the pitcher.

EVALUATING SPECIFIC PITCHES

The final problem-solving area that should be addressed involves reviewing the various difficulties that a particular pitcher may have with different pitches. Chart 10-2 provides an overview of how to evaluate problems attending to specific types of pitches. Chart 10-2, is divided into three elements—the pitch, the problem, and the possible cause of a particular problem.

Pitch	Problem	Cause
Drop ball	High in location	No angle over toes; stride is too long
	Lack of movement	Slow wrist snap; wrong angle
	Too slow	The wrist snap resembles a curve ball more than a drop ball
	Down and out movement	The stride is too short to create power
	Low in location	The release point is not within the box
Rise ball	Slow movement; no jump	Lazy wrist snap; not quick or complete
	Out of the strike zone	The stride is too short; late release
	Looks more like a curve ball	The thumb is snapping to the side instead of to the ground
	Always inside; the pitcher is having difficulty throwing an outside rise ball	Little or no closure of hips; the foot plant is incorrect
Curve ball	The ball drops more than it curves	The hand/wrist snap is coming over the top more than from the side
	Too high	The pitcher is bending at the elbow or pulling her hand away from her body on the release
	Little movement; ball over plate	The pitcher is throwing with her shoulder, not her wrist, and pulling her elbow away from her body
	The ball is too far off plate	The pitcher is leaning with her glove arm and dipping her shoulders

Chart 10-2: Analyzing specific pitches

Pitch	Problem	Cause
Screwball	Resembles rise ball	The pitcher's hips are getting in the way, allowing the backwards curve snap to occur
	Too slow	Lazy legs; the pitcher is throwing with all arm
	The pitcher is stepping too far to clear her hips	The buttocks push out, causing the pitcher to lose speed
	No movement	Lazy wrist snap; the pitcher is trying to throw only with her arm
Change-Up	Telegraphed	Slow arm speed; the pitcher's drive is too high, almost up
	High	The pitcher is not pushing the ball off early enough in the release box
	Too slow	The pitcher is not whipping her arm, which also telegraphs the pitch
	Too fast	Too much leg drive; the pitcher's stride may be too long

Chart 10-2 (cont.): Analyzing specific pitches

It should be emphasized that pitching problems are rarely caused by one single factor. A possibility always exists that one problem is being caused or set up by another problem. In pitching, as in hitting, one small problem often leads to another problem. Accordingly, the coach should focus on correcting one thing at a time and remember that the pitcher must feel, see, or be told what she is doing wrong in order to really be able to make a change or correction. The information provided in this chapter is just a starting point to help a coach solve some common pitching problems, since each pitcher is different. All factors considered, coaches and pitchers should remember to keep things simple when attempting to identify, evaluate, and address problems.

CHAPTER 11

Working on Drills

Drills are very worthwhile tools for softball coaches at all competitive levels. Properly executed drills can enable players to learn and maximize their playing skills. The following drills are designed to help a pitcher work on specific aspects of her delivery. Properly designed drills will break down individual skills within the pitching delivery to master the art.

DRILLS TO DEVELOP PROPER ROTATION

Rotation Drill

Rotation, or the opening and closing of the hips, should be a natural occurrence. The player should get down on her right knee (if right-handed) with her stride leg on the power line. Her navel should be pointing toward third base, while her plant foot should be at a 45-degree angle. The right arm should begin above the head, the left arm should be at the waist. As the player rotates back so that her navel is facing home plate, the left arm should be raised above the head, while the right arm should be pulled down to the waist. As she rotates toward third base, her arms should switch back to their original positions.

Mirror Drill

The pitcher should position herself in front of a mirror with her navel facing the mirror. She should put a piece of colored tape on her shirt to mark where her navel would be. Using a rolled up pair of socks as a ball, she should get in position to begin her pitching motion and go from Phase I to Phase II, all-the-while watching where her navel starts and finishes. This drill is designed to enable a pitcher to see whether she is staying opened or closed during her delivery and at her release.

Big Ball Drill

The pitcher may use any large ball (e.g., a basketball, a volleyball, or a soccer ball) for this drill. She should have a partner positioned 10 to 15 feet away and practice throwing the ball underhand. She should toss the ball and pivot, so she can feel the natural rotation of her hips.

Walk Through Drill

Players should be relaxed before beginning this drill. The pitcher should turn sideways and place her hands on her hips. Then, she should walk. She should feel her hips rotate open and closed every time she takes a step. This action is the same rotation she should have when pitching. Once she feels the natural rotation of her hips, she should actually pitch the ball by walking through the entire motion. Although this drill may feel awkward at first and may require several repetitions of walking into, during and after her motion, a pitcher will eventually master the necessary rotation movement.

Yardstick Drill

The pitcher should thread a yardstick or broomstick behind her back and in front of her elbows. Without using her arms, she should practice going from Phase I to Phase II. She should feel the closure or rotation of her hips.

Cement Drill

The player should stand with her feet shoulder-width apart and her knees flexed. She may bend her knees and twist her body, but her feet should remain in place as if she were standing in cement. The pitcher should then throw the ball as hard as possible. She should focus on getting power from the ground through her legs and deliver that power onto the ball.

Wall Drill

This drill should be done next to a padded wall or a fence that has been covered to protect the pitcher's arm. She should stand with her glove arm to the wall and practice Phase I and Phase II of her pitching motion. The wall will ensure that her glove arm goes out in front of her and not to the side. Once she demonstrates a basic mastery of the drill, she should then be required to actually pitch the ball.

DRILLS TO DEVELOP PROPER WRIST SNAP

Big-Ball Roll

Any large ball can be used for this drill. The pitcher should put the ball in the palm of her hand and then shoot it like she would a basketball. She should pay special attention to the feeling of the ball rolling off her fingertips and the snapping of her wrist. This drill helps many athletes see the correlation between various skills that are used in other sports.

Quick Wrist Snap

This drill involves placing tape on a ball around the horseshoes to enable the pitcher to watch the spin on the ball. Different taping for different pitches can assist in perfecting various pitches (e.g., a rise ball, a curve ball, a screw ball, and a drop ball). She should hold the ball in her pitching hand and place her glove hand in front of her pitching elbow. The pitcher should flip the ball in the air by flicking her wrist up, and continue flipping and catching the ball. Keeping her glove hand in front of her pitching elbow will help her make sure she is using her wrist, not her elbow, to flip the ball.

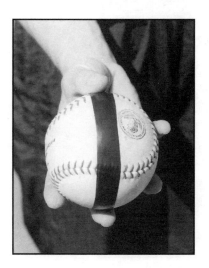

High Point

This drill is performed in the same manner as the quick wrist snap drill. In this drill, however, the pitcher should try to flip the ball higher with each toss, by utilizing a wrist snap—not her arm.

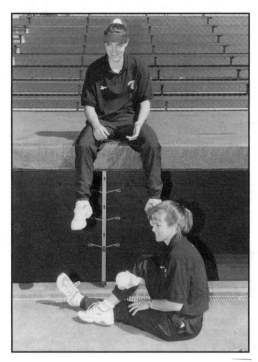

Pendulum Drill

The pitcher should stand on her power line, get the correct grip on the ball, and hold it next to her thigh. She should practice swinging her arm back and forth, trying to get it higher every time she passes the release point. After a predetermined number of practice swings, she should release the ball when her arm comes forward. One of the primary points that should be emphasized to the pitcher is that she should remain relaxed while performing the drill, somewhat like a "rag doll."

DRILLS TO DEVELOP PROPER ARM CIRCLES

Reach for the Sky

The pitcher should practice her drive, reaching as high as she can going into Phase I. She should ensure that her arm is not locked; it is relaxed and loose. As her arm reaches its highest point, she can freeze her arm to see where it is.

Reach for the Coach

The coach should stand on a chair next to the pitcher and hold up her hand. The pitcher should practice her drive and arm extension, reaching for the coach's hand as she goes into Phase I.

T Drill

The player should stand with her arms stretched out to the side so that her body is in the shape of a "T." She should swing her arms as if tracing the bottom half of a circle—first pushing them forward and then pulling them back, while remembering to snap her wrist. Once she has practiced the basic movement involved in the drill, the pitcher should progress to a point where she is actually throwing the ball so that she can see where the ball goes and hopefully the spin on the ball.

Wall Drill for Pitching Arm

This drill can be done using a padded wall or a fence that is covered to protect the pitcher's arm. The drill begins by having the pitcher get down on one knee with her pitching arm adjacent to the wall and practice Phase I and Phase II. The wall will keep her arm moving straight ahead instead of out to the side. Subsequently, the drill can progress to a point where the pitcher actually pitches the ball and utilizes her entire delivery.

Follow-Through Drill

The drill begins by having the pitcher go through her pitching motion and follow-through. Her coach stands in front of her and observes her movements. As the pitcher finishes her motion, the coach should throw balls back at her feet. This step forces the pitcher to get into position to field the ball after her follow-through. This drill is designed to force a pitcher to focus on where her balance is immediately following her delivery (particularly after having thrown specific pitches).

DRILLS TO DEVELOP PROPER BALANCE

Phase I and Phase II

The coach should either use a string or draw a line in the dirt in front of the mound to represent the power line. The pitcher should set up on the mound. When the coach yells "Phase I," the pitcher should go to the Phase I position checking foot placement and balance. The coach may then yell "Phase II"—a signal to the pitcher to go to the Phase II position. As the pitcher goes to each position, close attention should be paid to whether or not she has maintained a proper level of balance.

Phase I

Phase II

Phase II

One-Knee Drill

The pitcher should get down on her push-off knee and get into the Phase I position. Her plant foot should be set on the power line. She should begin the drill with the ball held above her head and bring it through the rest of the motion, taking care to remain balanced. The coach may help her maintain her balance by placing her hands on the pitcher's head (to provide a steady degree of support) while she is performing the pitching motion.

Carie Dever-Boaz is the Head Women's Softball Coach at the University of Arkansas. Before assuming her present position in 1995, Dever-Boaz was the pitching coach at the University of South Carolina, where her pitching staff earned national recognition. Under Dever-Boaz, one of her pitchers earned NCAA Division I All-American Honors in 1995. A graduate of Fresno State, Dever-Boaz had an extraordinary career as a member of the Bulldog softball team, earning Division I All-American honors three times as a pitcher and third baseman. In the process, she led Fresno State to four consecutive NCAA World Series appearances. After graduation, she played for the National Fastpitch Association's Stars in the women's professional softball league. As a frequent instructor at camps and a much sought after speaker at clinics, Dever-Boaz has also produced three softball instructional videos, including "Set Them up and Sit Them Down" with Karen Sanchelli, "How to Pitch in Softball," and "Drills, Drills, and More Drills." She lives with her husband, Bruce, and son, Max, in Fayetteville, Arkansas.

Sally Tippett Rains is a freelance writer who has written several sports books, including *Youth Baseball: A Coach's and Parent's Guide* (with Wendell Kim, the third base coach for the Boston Red Sox) and *Drills and Skills for Youth Basketball* (with Rich Grawer, the athletic director at Clayton High School in Clayton, Missouri). Her background as a writer includes working as a sports reporter at KMOX Radio in St. Louis and writing several articles for *The Sporting News*. She also wrote *Playing On His Team* with her husband, Rob Rains. They live with their two sons, B.J. and Mike, in St. Louis, Missouri.